It's Cold Outside

By Cameron Macintosh

Let's see how animals stay snug when it's cold outside.

Some animals seek cosy spots.

Other animals have thick coats or oily down when it gets cold.

The oil keeps this duck's down dry.

This cow has a thick coat.

Snow falls, but these cows don't get cold.

When it's cold,
a bat eats more food.

This adds weight around its body,
which keeps out the cold.

Brown bears have a thick coat.

They add weight, too.

Brown bears browse around for a good cave.

They lie down and enjoy a deep sleep till spring.

Here is a bear that found a great cave!

This mouse made a cosy nest.

The nest is in a tree,
high off the cold ground.

The mouse's pointy nose pokes out.

Some animals keep lots of food in their homes. Then they won't have to go outside.

This animal can stuff lots of nuts in its mouth!

These insects fight the cold by staying close to each other.

Then they fly around and go to a hot place.

This insect can't wait to join the crowd.

Pets enjoy staying snug, too!

This hound gets cosy on the couch.

CHECKING FOR MEANING

1. What do brown bears do in their caves in winter? *(Literal)*
2. What stops the duck's down from getting wet? *(Literal)*
3. Why is the animal on page 11 stuffing nuts into its mouth? *(Inferential)*

EXTENDING VOCABULARY

down	What are the two different meanings of the word *down* used in this book?
browse	What does the word *browse* mean? What is another way to say *browse*?
hound	What letters in the word *hound* make the /ow/ sound? What is a hound? What is another word the author could have used?

MOVING BEYOND THE TEXT

1. This book describes the different ways animals stay snug when it is cold outside. What are some ways people stay warm and snug when it is cold outside?
2. Have you ever snuggled up with a pet at home? How did that make you feel?
3. The animals in the book feel a change in the weather and prepare for winter. What are some ways you might prepare for winter?
4. Have you ever seen snow? If yes, what does snow feel like? If no, what do you imagine snow feels like?

TIME TO WRITE

Write from the point of view of one of the animals in the text. Winter is starting, and you have to get ready. What do you do?

PRACTICE WORDS

oily

down

brown

couch

crowd

outside

around

out

ground

cows

how

cow

found

pointy

mouse's

oil

enjoy

mouse

can't

browse

mouth

it's

won't

join

hound

let's

don't